Natural Disaster, That She Was

Silence Staats

Presentation by *BookLeaf Publishing*

Web: www.bookleafpub.com

E-mail: info@bookleafpub.com

ISBN: 978-93-95755-71-9

First edition 2022

*To my biggest supporters; my family,
friends, and the unconditional communities
who more than patiently wait for my next
pieces to come together in untimely
fashions.*

*This collection is dedicated to the people
who have never shied away from my
temperament, the strange ideas I produce
and have only encouraged and loved my
fluid tones and endless creativity.*

*You hold and inspire me more than
anything.*

ACKNOWLEDGEMENT

There are not enough words to describe how grateful I am for all the wonderful influences in my life. To my mom, my dad for always encouraging any creative process that my brothers and I have expressed an interest in. For always being my biggest supporters, even though I don't share my writing much. I love you both so much and wish I could give you more than the world.

To Anna, and Andrew, who glanced first at my hand-written words and found nothing other than compliments to surface, and for giving advice I can only apply to my life, when I decided I was ready.

Ary and Quinn; both of you have supported all of silly pieces I have ever produced, because it came from the authentic parts of my center. Thank you for being my undivided support, confidants, and greatest friends. I adore both of you to the fullest. That belief in me, in my writing, has created this very collection, and you two are the heart of it.

To my high-school English teachers for always encouraging the style of writing I tried to keep hidden. Thank you for never silencing my voice, or my stories.

PREFACE

creativity is my compulsion, and compulsion is what makes the artist.

seedling

the creators, nestled me in their hands
turning my energy with a swipe of separate
wrists, trembling
clockwise and lathered with affection,
whispering amongst of all the intensity i will
come to consume and give away -
my soul spinning in subtle stirs
as they wonder what i could use,
how they could shape my being
"within reason,"
to form a shell, a carcass, a body, a home, to
embodiment, a sculpture, and there -
there, i began to form, to come together
(for descent)
with a smooth touch, a low quiver, and only a
fraction of guidance,
hints of lavender and rain -
earth-reigned tones,
impressed by the wind and coloured hues,
shaped, in the exact image of a tree
with the marks running along my thighs,
reminiscent with the familiar strikings of
deepened bark -
a wide and full cage - rings and rings (stumped)
and my arms, faulted as branches,

with the constant need to predominantly sway
back and forth
- planting both feet into the ground, burying
myself into soil and
roots that only force forward (vital for
consumption)
the same ground that sinks underneath as i cross
fields barefoot
the steady pulse
the need, the desire, my desires -
to curl within myself each winter and unfold
again after the harshest of storms (wrecked and
havocked)

and mother, mother-earth, mother, mother -
she's calling my name now,
she wants me to stretch and come home -
        mother,
        mother,
        mother, mother, my mother
        calling for me, "silence-"

satisfied with my image, make, my embedded
journey,
valued and sprouted into the soul -
my creators each placed a kiss on my eyelids,
planted those seeds in my mind, and sent me
home.

holistic rituals

there is something almost feral -
animalistic by nature
in the way i crave to turn
under the elegant rituals of the night skies -
to bathe in the explosions universes,
salted and relaxed
praising the past versions of selves,
under full moons
with lithe and sanctioned movement,
in the middle of forests
to any tempo provided, (if intended)
entertaining my gaze, and my gaze solely -
in the blurred reflection of the river,
the ends of my dress tousled, smudged
(smelling of sweetened grasses)
rolling around with mouthfuls of dirt,
synchronized with the changes around my
scenery,
in the foggy haze of late nights and early
mornings
(as close as i'll ever come to dancing in the
cloud)

whispers of -

one more spoonful
of that havocked spice
dusted my bloody lips,
knotted in the back of my throat, charred
persisted along the tops of tables, decorated
counters,
and my fingertips -
"to be purified, protected,"
and here i sit, tapping my feet -
petrified at the barricaded doorways, boarded
and blocked -
the low vibration of your voice shifting through
the small spaces, proclaimed
that i will be struck, stuck, dirtied
until i prove my devotion, my innocence strung
[whispers of witch, witch, witch]
- leaping and cruel,
until the bowl is finished, and i cannot croak
[whispers of witch, witch, witch]
you unbuckled each chain, broke every barrier
[soaked with my lineage]
announced your way into the dim room,
scattered that i was sheltered and resurrected, at
such a barren offer
[whispers of witch, witch, witch]

reaching to brush the hair from my face
crouched, levelled, lowered - whispered -
don't choke, don't choke, don't choke
and if there was only one sentiment i echoed, it
was that you were coming down with me,
i grabbed the back of your head, in disguise,
gingerly moving it to rest against mine -
in hymn, asking for forgiveness, spitting out
verses together -
burrowing in my own defenses, to calm you
down,
before breaking your nose
felled -
pushing to my power, to abolish everything you
held sacred, and every word you used in turn
against me,
drawing pressure on your chest, lowering myself
-
regurgitating everything i was forced to swallow,
straight into the back of your throat,
with suffocating intention this time,
mingled with my anger, disposition and your
blood
the whispers, invaded the room
- various of generations screaming -
joined by my own scratched surface
"witch, witch, witch-"

stains, they don't seem to wash away

blackberries bruise the outline of your lips,
matching perfectly with the colour stained
underneath my seated and sleepless eyes -
they state it's because you talk too much -
a consequence of your own action, meddling
your way into conversations you have no
business holding stakes in,
(that's what they say, anyways)

the same way they gripe to tell you that i'm too
observant, too quick to motion - too quick to the
call of busy - that i cannot sleep, maimed, only
by my own caged insomnia and fuckery, unable
to doze, from the events i have witnessed by my
own accord -
that i see things that i shouldn't, unnoticed by the
flocked gazes -
that i see things that aren't there, aren't mine -
that we would be fatal -
weaving that web,
and perhaps the bruising i spot on you, is that of
my imagination
(that's what they say, anyways)

as you spilled, with that tenor, range and tone,
i knew you could command an army,
with the most mundane collection of words,
glory flashing through your expression
you realize they were right
you spoke, and i watched -
kneading our pile of leftover branches together,
hung on by nothing in particular
as you mumble something about spewing
protections, the healing prosperities of the
blackberries, your bruises came to darken and
spread -
as we both tasted the same flavours in different
variations, in different rotations -

discoveries, plenty

my personality is unappealing
(not to those exceptional and understood few)
still, after twenty-four years
i am no longer entirely sure who i present
spirited as,
after finding myself tangled in many society
swallowed faults
(shallow and insignificant)
yet, i struggle to find any piece of myself
in piles of individually shredded papers
perpetually arguing back and forth with the
saturated ink,
that discolours my fingertips for days on end-
begging to feel preserved in expressing myself
freely, authentic, somehow, someway,
to sing in a room full of people - even though i
cannot carry a tune
to wrap myself in warmth,
and in bundles of comfort,
to be held, grazed, folded - to be decorated by
my own hands and image.

scratches

there's something in the back of my mouth
take your hand, it's right here -
no, not there, it's right here,
can you feel it? tell me that you're experiencing
the same perplexed motions that i am?
that somewhere, somehow in your own body
in your frame, you feel the very same pressures
parallel to my own - reassure my worrying state
that i'm not the only one feeling out of place
within
this and with these lucid vibrations -
and that scratch, the scratching that is lining the
very
back of my throat in this exact moment
(entwined with your hands now, can you feel it
this time?)
that cannot be eased or subdued, extinguished -
it's always evident, paralyzing any sound at the
only of worst moments
when i long to convict, convince and paint
myself as a strong
and powerful individual - scratching, burning,
as if i am
continuously swallowing things i shouldn't be
and

dismounting myself with the boxed match-sticks
(brand; wild honeys, for small cigars),
swallowing them and the flames whole -
torching my insides

i'd dislodge my own jaw, if it meant driving this
feeling away.

my victories, they're within

if i had succeeded in halting, tarnishing, pausing
my life in those impulsive moments
i would have missed plenty-
(and the more they would have mourned)
i would have skipped those explosive sunrises,
late, sleepless nights,
where my energy exceeds me-
seeing my name in print,
on the other side of eyes that aren't my mine
taking the very risks that had before left me
frigid and locked in place
(and i am reaping in my own rewards)
unraveling pieces of my soul
finding that helpless child that sits between
between my rib-cage,
and hugging her
insisting she was enough, in all ways, every
single one.
i have fully fed her, allowing her to take reign,
to walk hand-in-hand with her, and lead her into
the experience of healing, whispering soothing
revelations, and reminding her that she deserves
more than creation itself//
i would have missed turns around the sun,
shedding my previous poses

reflecting on my traumas,
finding my power, by god, i am divine, and a
thousand other things wrapped into one body - i
can't ever forget that.
i would have lost on the laughter that i not only
produced, but the laughter that came from my
depths, laughter that i had to rediscover -
i had been running on isolation and ruining
thoughts for so long,
now, i do not blindly jump over any chances of
simply learning to be,
finding contentment in each obstacle i run into,
fully embracing all of my heavy feelings instead
of evading them. i was meant to witness my
worst moments,
to grow find that i was my own reason to
continue, my own reason to stay, to keep trying,
that i had to, i had to keep moving, constantly
breathing - i owed it to myself, to give it one last
try, to try and love myself
even when the world seemed like one vast,
dangerous, swallowing and unknown black hole
and guess what?

i did it.

and i more than desperately want everyone to
achieve the same.

everything else can sit and wait

there's something delicate playing on the
morning radio,
my movements are light
and these thoughts are slowly burning -
adjusting to the somber hues draped around my
curtains,
dragging my fingers through various spreads
humming my way through every chorus as my
legs tangle in cold sheets,
simplified,
knowing there's a kettle waiting to flicker
and a warm bowl of steeled oats -
(cinnamon, blueberries, and stained with honey)
my chosen tea-leaves tucked under a broken
glass
(marjoram, this mourn)
there is no rush, no need for adjustment,
i could lay still for hours, in this semi-sable
room
neglecting whatever has to play tomorrow,
to whatever is unfolding outside -
only give in to myself (barefoot)

on and on i take the time to laugh with my
reflection,
(i love watching that smile widen)
watching her move back and forth through the
steam in the mirror,
drops of water collecting in to a small puddle on
the floor in the middle of the room
in no rush to clothe, or do much of anything at
all,
except admiration, and whispers of no substance
(those are my favorite kind)
stitching whatever needs that need to be softly
felt and cradled for the day,
controlling the only thing i know how
(myself and my responses)
and allowing everything else to only pass
through -
and never settle.
my hands, were created to nurture
and the rest of the world can wait,
i have to tend to my self, my body, my soils first.

they have big things planned
for -

i am the daughter of all the things they have
failed to eradicate,
[and that alone is a thing to cherish]
molded by the ancient(s)
and wisdom-reigned spirits
holding a thousand tongues, experiences and
versions, unknowingly in my streams - in every
strand of hair, holds another piece of my
extraction, my lines -
i have been curated with a drummed heart, more
love to handle, and empathy that knows only
stepping on bounds and reaching, reaching,
reaching
fated to spin in a thousand directions and ingest
a thousand different emotions and pathways,
always unmarked and blinded, overwhelmed by
opportunity,
aligned with the inevitable stir to find my bliss,
and although i have found a thousand other
things, and have worked myself endlessly,
without a break-
they're not finished with me, not yet
and i am so ready for what is meant to find me
next

tug-of-war

she appears on occasion
(once or twice a month now, usually for a couple
days)
with a weighted/whining presence
promptly tossing herself on the edge of my bed
just before i fully wake
listening to the slow drumming of my pulse,
rocketing as she begins to reach for my hands
waking me with a quick pinch -
dread -
i'm used to her visitations now,
but still weary
every-single-time she announces herself
she's the destructive person i once was
had been, had fueled, had embodied and here
she sits,
with the quick reminder that she can still
puppeteer my mood
finding her way back, and through my body
without a map,
reminiscing about our old times, our old
thoughts, our old habits
with a bottle of pills in one hand, a drink in the
other,
both uncapped -

and i know she's concealing a few choice blades
underneath her sleeves
 - if i wanted another taste, another trial, she'd
allow it -
but no matter what she says, or manages to pull
in temptations, i'm steadfast in my decisions to
pull as well - and she's the one ending up with
rope burns.

re-done tapestries

where did i last leave those embroidery scissors?
because i am left hanging by another thread, a
single strand,
and i'd like to let myself down
one more time
so it be
before diving into an age-old sewing kit
(passed through hands before mine, and to be
passed on after)
searching for another colour that hasn't yet been
through my own use -
that hasn't been implanted in my tapestry,
threaded through my lips,
splicing my fingers back together when they
unravel -
looking for another strand to showcase my
artistry,
my tremor-ridden hands can patchwork, over
and over again
whenever i am feeling less than worthy,
when i have been an object of a(   )
when my worlds are starved, tilted and
comatose,
everything feels elaborate and suffocating

when i can no longer stand the sight of myself
any longer,
of my body,
as hard as i might try -
my grip re-works, re-patches
restarts with each fiber and steel needle that
pierces through my skin,
riddled with gentle and fulfilling affirmations
attached, and bonding the other thousands of
colours together once more
tied with a finalized knot, and expert precision
happier with the person i have established with
my own tender and loved intentions.

she is art.

sugarcoated

i'm tired of censoring my trauma,
sugarcoating it -
so that your pill is easier to swallow
because mine
still gets lodged into my throat,
expanding each time i try to gasp, to grasp
when i try to release everything i have inhaled -
[maximum capacity]
one more attempted whisper,
and i'll no longer suffocate.

i am a mixture of tragedies and disaster
[room temperature]
topped carelessly with crushed foam -
acidic to the tongue,
leaving a tart film in the mouths that have
opened for a sample -
[i won't speak much, no]
and my recipe is not up for discussion,
because it has been handcrafted with anger and
bitterness,
to my frequency, to my taste, to my panic,
and to the ways i have pushed my own body in
pursuit of staying quiet and contempt.

i'll fall back tonight, into my pillow
knowing that i have torn the system apart
because while my throat is constantly
threatening to silence my delivery,
my brain is actively working through different
methods of communication
and they all settle well before my eyes close.

cosmic, at the same time

i opened myself to the endless ideas of the cosmos,
the higher vibrations,
the pull to search for something more,
something beyond myself, beyond my physical
abilities,
the earth began to shudder as i laid myself on the
uneven grounds -
hypnotized by the onset of stars, and the muddled
atmosphere above,
as they rearranged and painted themselves into an
ethereal portrait for myself,
and perhaps for anyone else who happened to be
sprawled out,
under the same night skies, at exactly the same time
as i was,
perhaps on the cold cement, or a rooftop so high that
they could dance themselves straight into the stars,
or maybe they were wondering down the emptied
streets,
walking in the middle of the road, struck by the
stardust that filled while everyone else deemed sleep,
and only dreamt of the ordinary
all the while, the galaxy danced underneath our
hooded eyelids - making the impossible happen with
no more effort than it takes to automatically breathe,
to think, to feel, to be -

and you

what you deem as your own imperfections,
i breathe as a work of art.

art is not catered to be perfect -
and that is what makes each piece desirable in
someone else's mind.

art is undiscovered beauty,
and you,
you inspire every attachment of my being.

maybe, i

maybe if i stopped screaming my sorrows into
aching pillows,
the muted moonlight and those scorched,
steaming showers -
and instead fought with all my anxieties,
swallowed my self-aimed guilt
breaking through those damned insecurities that
are worked into my core-
and gathered the courage to look directly into
the writhing sunlight
collect those fated sun-burns
[titled icarus]
to continue to navigate through my locked jaw,
to turn my off-key wine whispers into a strong
melody that punctuates perfectly with the fired
rhythm running through my chest -
that echoed through the universe,
and to have people run - to run into my turmoil
citing that they understand every emotion i once
tried to deny
to relate on the memories i've desperately tried
to keep hidden
to reminisce in the silence and worries that have
resulted in my misplaced violence, and this odd
hatred for myself -

maybe i'd feel less overwhelmed, less alone, less
barren,
and less likely to tear myself apart in those
ridden, and bare nights.

shed that mindset

the prospect of
"fake it until you make it -"
has led me unable to identify any emotions
that i may now feel -
it doesn't work.
why do i have to fake this?
why can't i expel my woes
and simply have bad days?
why is it necessary that i hide behind a smile?
because it makes other people uncomfortable?
because they'll start to feel worried and
concerned?
imagine how i feel.
misery,
misery,
misery lives within me,
a pestering roommate
and i'm exhausted of pretending it doesn't.

i fight back -

you inhaled me whole,
off-key and with a glass of your favoured drink
[making an absolute mess]
pressing your tongue between my teeth,
listing off my flaws as they appear.

you echoed my own blemishes
as you managed your way through my mind
and my body -
blood belonging on the napkin in your lap
you had no need for those daintily wrapped
utensils,
digging through the scraps of my soul,
foraging for yourself the very pieces i never
truly enclosed
[you didn't remember to read my fine-print did
you?]

submissive, they ask of women
[my name, a disguise]
for women,
to remain open and available
- for only the things that appease and pleasure
them
dreadful, and downright pathetic

keep breaking me apart with your filthy hands
because i know that i will be leaving you with a
sour taste in your mouth
and maggots rotting in your extremities, as
intended.

waiting for me

he stands in the middle of the road
cloaked by nothing less than the shadows
which have befallen his sickly figure,
while he whistles the same haunting tune
without even a falter
underneath the shards of broken glass
his hands shoved away steadily in his pockets,
patiently waiting.

always,
his eyes flicker to the heavily curtained
frames of a broken window,
knowing he is still uninvited.

his watch, it no longer works
the sound had faded months ago
when he decided my time had expired.

in a force of habit i pull the fabric back
delivering the same soundless laugh
we have both grown to anticipate
as he gives a sheepish wave
the corners of his lips unfurling from his
trademark scowl
asking when i will finally be accompanying him.

he waits with the same polished expression
rocking on the broken steps
of the vacant house across the street
already having finished with his previous list
from the morning.

if only they knew
death would forever be waiting on me.

and you, again

i hope one day
you see how thoroughly
incredible and striking you
are - even when it
feels like the world
is crumbling against
you in quick succession.
you, you are evidence
of strength, resilience, and
the ability to overcome
in spite of every
obstacle they
have thrown
at you. you were created
to withhold. and i think
you're the most beautiful
thing i have ever laid my eyes on.
in a multitude of ways.

try it, see what happens

you will not silence me, keep me mum, still,
unexpressed, dull of even obedient. i am
not willing to bite my bruised tongue for
you any longer - [not anymore] - not even if
you shoved your hands into my mouth and
scraped the lining of my throat raw, until i
choke on my own blood. my blurry vision
will find yours through the howling of my
pain and torment - [a pompous sound that
will follow you everyday] - my blood will
drip down your arm, and along my
outstretched neck, teething on your knuckles.
it will spill from the corners of my mouth
with a rasp, showering you with one last
parting gift even as my life slips from me
- [you will remain stigmatized and haunted] -
i will linger in the stains on the floor,
embedding myself into the treads of your shoes,
always unsteady through the whispers on
your mind, my outraged tucked away
underneath your fingernails -
- [and the only way to get rid of my evidence,
is to peel each one off, with your own teeth] -

i'd take every last bit

i've crawled (with expedited bruises) from
situations, areas and locale that would wreck
absolute havoc on anyone's being -
dis-alignment, this wasn't meant for us -
truth-be-told i'd rather it have been me, instead
of the masses… instead of it being someone i
knew, someone dear and close (these thoughts
make my stomach quake, and i'm trembling) -
someone i knew … having the same thought
process, ideations, disassociations, the emptiness
that i have had to navigate -
i'd do it a thousand times over to erase that kind
of control, to erase that kind of pain, the kind of
pain that a core could never truly forget
a pain that influences fever dreams, panic, a
handful of disastrous choices, addictions,
mutilations, pain that results in people being
buried way too young, way before a life is
allowed to blossom,
(i was almost there, my own body thrown into
the cold ground).
i would carry every moment, memory and mark
from their skin, and introduce it as my own, if it
meant that no one else would injure sleepless
nights, constantly plagued by shadows across the

ceilings as they wonder what they had done,
what they could've done differently, what they
did to deserve this …
i'd take it all, and leaving everything else,
unscathed, without that heavy weight,
unbothered and give them a chance to know
exactly how irreplaceable they are, what a gift
having their soul around is -
to bestow them with even a single moment of
serenity, silence, healing and laughter.
and i'd deal with it. i know that i can survive and
overcome the basis of the greedy, devious, evil
and unkempt,
and still manage to find the very depths of
myself and achieve lightness in the process. it's
something that no one should ever be robbed of
experiencing, and i'd give it all away,
and openly if i knew how…
if i could take my hands, and somehow release
every singe - i'd do it. i fucking would